Shannon Hurst Lane

The Definitive Guide to Travel Writing

Zala Lane

Zala Lane Publishing

Published by Zala Lane Productions, a division of Lane Enterprises, PO Box 437, Zachary, LA 70791

First Published by Zala Lane Productions,

A division of Lane Enterprises

First Printing, June 2007

ISBN 978-0-6151-4987-5

Copyright © Shannon Hurst Lane, 2007

All Rights Reserved

Special thanks to my family and friends for their support and assistance during this journey.

Table of Contents

Tourist Boards

There are so many travel courses out there promising free trips and no-cost vacations for life. These courses may cost hundreds of dollars and talk of fame and riches. That's not what I'm about. I want you to know the truth about travel writing and would rather see you purchase some good luggage for all those research trips you are about to take, than to throw away your dollars.

This guide will lead you in the right direction and get you on your way to being a travel writer. This book has areas for you to take notes, and blank pages at the end to write about your press trips. But, there are some hard truths you must know. Its not always glamourous and it can be tough to make a living, but it can be done with hard work and persistence. I would not suggest giving up your day job. In fact, I still have another job that provides me with benefits which being a freelancer does not provide.

So, get that passport ready!

What makes me think I am qualified to tell you about becoming a travel writer? I actually fell into travel writing accidentally.

I started travel writing in my twenties after I took a vacation with my family and the trip went awry. I used this experience to help other parents at my office get value for their time and money. Nothing is worse than spending thousands of dollars on a dream trip, only to find out that the hotel is not in the best shape and amenities are not what was advertised. I also started a newsletter called The Traveling Firefighter, which now has more than 100,000 readers and is sent to fire stations all over the US. The website and newsletter was even featured on a nationally sydicated daytime talk show! (*The Caroline Rhea Show, October 2002*)

I learned everything about travel writing from the Internet and you can too. All it takes is a desire to learn and this inexpensive guide. Since learning the ins and outs of travel writing, I have been interviewed on BBC Radio in the UK and The Trip Chicks in the Southern US. My articles have appeared in MSNBC.com, San Antonio AT HOME, Louisiana Homes & Gardens, and Tall magazines, websites and newspapers around the globe. I was even the travel editor for Baton Rouge Weddings Magazine, a 148 page high gloss magazine.

There are so many resources available. Some are free or a minimal cost. When I first started travel writing, I made around $100 per month. If I had all the information in this guide back then, I could have made more than $500 a month with minimal effort. Not a bad supplement to an annual income.

So, I want to give you some advice before you step into the travel writing world. I cannot stress this enough, - don't quit your day job. It is unrealistic to expect a six figure salary as a travelwriter. Yes, there are a few individuals who have managed this feat, but it takes time and effort to establish yourself in this industry.

You CAN travel the world. You just have to believe in yourself.

The World is a book, and those who do not travel read only a page.

Saint Augustine

Writing Terms

Assignment – An article or story assigned to you by an editor.

Byline – Your name. Not all publications assign bylined articles. You want a bylined article.

Clip – A published sample of your work. It can be a photocopy or a scanned digital copy. This is also called a "tear sheet."

Comp – Sometimes writers on assignment get compensated or reduced rates on lodging, attractions, and meals. Be sure to check with your publication's guidelines before accepting comps. Some newspapers and magazines will not accept "comped" trips.

Copyright – A copyright is your right of ownership for anything you write. It can be formally copyrighted at the US Copyright Office. See www.copyright.gov

Credits – A list of your published articles or works.

CVB – Convention and Visitor's Bureau.

Deadline – This is the last possible moment you are allowed to turn in an article.

Kill fee – This is a pre-negotiated fee paid if you are assigned an article and the editor doesn't use it. It can be 25-100% or a set amount. Be sure to have this in your contract.

On spec – This is short for "on speculation." An editor may respond to a query accepting the article on spec. This means you write the article with no guarantee that it will be printed.

Payment – Contracts state monetary terms usually as payment on publication or as payment on acceptance. It is preferable to receive payment on acceptance. You will be paid sooner, if at all.

Press trip – This is a research or familiarization(fam) trip sponsored by a tourism board or public relations company. There are group and individual trips. Most group trips include transportation, accommodations, meals, and activities. Individual trips usually do not include transportation. Be advised: Not all publications accept articles generated from press trips. Check writer's guidelines.

PR – This stands for public relations. A PR company can represent various clients in the travel and tourism industry.

Query – Your pitch of an article to an editor. This is how you get assignments. If a publication states that it wants postal queries only, then do not send an email query.

Reprint – Selling an article over and over. You can sell the same article to non-competing publications if you retain your copyrights.

Rights – This should be negotiated in your contract. Never sell all rights unless the money is significant. Even then, I do not recommend this route.

SASE – Self-addressed stamped envelope.

Sidebar – An addition to article containing tips or bulleted items (Ex. If You Go).

Simultaneous Submission – The act of submitting the same article pitch to more than one editor.

Word count – An editor may assign a 1,500 word article. This is your word count and should be closely followed because editors leave specific room in publications for certain article lengths.

Writer's guidelines – These are rules of submission a publication wants writers to follow. Each publication has its own writer's guidelines. It is advisable to adhere to these rules.

Write down other terms you come across here:

Travel, in the younger sort, is a part of education; in the elder, a part of experience.

Francis Bacon

Finding Your Niche

To be successful in the travelwriting industry, you need to find the place where you fit. Ask yourself the following questions and write your answer down in the space provided. Use another sheet, if necessary:

Where do I travel on vacation? Do I like beaches or mountains? Domestic or international? Am I a cruise aficianado?

What activities do I like to do when I travel? Golf? Go hiking? Do I enjoy fishing? Museums? History? Adventure? Spas?

What is my age group?

Do I have children? Do they reside at home? Am I able to travel at the spur of the moment or do I need a few week's or month's notice?

Do I own a Recreational Vehicle(RV) or go camping often?

What is my income? Am I a luxury or budget traveler?

There are so many types of travel writers out there. It is important to write about what you know. You can write about what you love to do, and if you do it often, you are already an expert. You just need to share your experience and knowledge with others.

There are many travel writing categories or genres. The following are the most popular:

Luxury

Cruises

Adventure

Student

Family

Senior

Business

Golf Getaways

Romantic

Destination Weddings

Spa

Wine and Food (Epicurean)

The first step in deciding which genre you specialize is to find the kind you most enjoy. You can even become an expert on a specific area. The best place to start is your own backyard. That's how I started. My initial articles were published in my local paper and were about weekend getaways from there. Become an expert on your area and you will have set the foundation for your travel writing career.

My writing is a combination of three elements. The first is travel: not travel like a tourist, but travel as exploration. The second is reading literature on the subject. The third is reflection.

Ryszard Kapuscinski

Queries

A query is your introduction to an editor or publication. Consider it your calling card. Many writers work long and hard on their queries. But what exactly is a query? It is a question, or in writing terms a pitch to write an article. Queries are different for magazine articles than for guidebooks. A publisher would require a one to two page query letter along with sample chapters or an outline for any guidebook consideration. Article writing is different. Short concise queries are what have been most successful for me. For example, I sent a query to a big name magazine that resulted in a phone call of interest thirty minutes after I sent it. This was the email:

Hi (XXXXX) –

I'll be in Ireland next month for a week. I plan on visiting Celtic Seaweed Day Spa in Sligo, attending an exclusive Yeats themed dinner, and many places between Shannon and Dublin. Are you interested in a destination article or a hotel review? Please let me know word counts and deadlines. My clips are available at shannonlane.com.

Thanks,

Shannon

I always have my signature including full name, email address, phone number, website, and a list of writing credits.

Here is another successful query that generated a very nice clip for my portfolio. This was a new publication:

Hi (XXXX) –

Would your publication be interested in a roundup article of hotels suitable for your readers? There are a few hotels in the US with rooms that cater to tall individuals. Thanks for your time.

Shannon

(signature line with personal details)

The editor of Tall Magazine emailed me the next day offering a 1500 word assignment that ended up being a cover story. Who knew there were so many hotels that offered special rooms for taller travelers? I was so excited to get a contributor copy in the mail with my check.

I've spoken with many editors over the years and we have discussed likes and dislikes when receiving queries. Editors are busy and want you to get to the point in the queries. The more specific the query, the better. Don't just tell them the destination, let them know where you are staying, what attractions would be of benefit to their readers? Don't pitch a cruise story to a golf magazine unless it features a driving range on the ship. Why would an adventure magazine care about a spa resort unless it is set in an adventurous location and offers sports and activities geared towards its readers.

Use this area for brainstorming:

Query Tips (The Lane Method):

Familiarize yourself with the publication. Read the magazine. Know the sections and which department is the best fit for your query.

Read the writer guidelines.

Think about your story angle before sending a query. You can't just tell an editor where you are going, you have to sell an idea to they just can't live without.

Try and make sure they have not done a similar piece in the last two years.

IMPORTANT. Make the query short and to the point. You need to exude confidence and professionalism. Editors are busy and they can weed out the pros from the hacks by the length and the content of the query.

Refer the editor to your online resume or writer's website for writing samples and credits. This will help cut the length of your query and the editor will not be put-off by attachments. If the editor is really interested in your pitch, they *may* take a look at your work via your site. Many may not even look at the site if they like your pitch. They are just too busy.

Examples of writer's websites:

www.shannonlane.com

www.jenleo.com

www.angusjjbell.com

www.cindyloudale.com

www.countrymatters.net

www.richarduhlhorn.com

www.parkersnyder.com

www.deevandyk.com

Always list your credits in your signature line, if you have any. This is another way to make an editor's life easier. They will be able to see where you have been published before.

TIP: I use http://www.homestead.com as a host for my website. It is easy to set up, inexpensive, and you can register your domain name for a professional look. They have many templates suitable for the writing profession. If your domain name is already taken, use your initials.

Be sure to keep track of queries and assignments, as well as contact information. Editors change at publications all the time. You want to protect yourself and any assignments you may have, just in case your contact has left the publication.

Here is a worksheet to follow when sending out queries.

Name of Publication:_____

Name/Address Sent to:_____

Date Sent:_____

Accepted?_____

Due Date:_____Word Count:_____

Contract Signed?_____Amount_____

Article Premise:_____

_____

_____

_____

_____

_____

_____

_____

_____

Completed?_____

Accepted by editor?_____

Payment Received_____

I love absolutely everything about my job. I get to meet loads of really nice people and travel around the world.

Jamelia

What is a press trip?

A press trip is a sponsored press junket put on by CVBs, Public Relations(PR) companies, destinations, resorts and Tourism Boards. These usually include accommodations, meals, transportation, and some activities. There are GROUP press trips and INDIVIDUAL press trips. Securing transportation on an individual trip is usually much harder.

How do I find out about these trips?

Many PR Companies schedule group press trips throughout the year. Sometimes they are listed on individual company websites, or they can be found through different writers' services, such as

www.TravelWriters.com

www.MediaKitty.com

www.ATMSTravelNews.com

www.GoTravelNews.com

Or through other professional organizations.

How do I qualify?

PR Companies list their offerings on the abovementioned websites. They also send out personal invitations to a large number of writers. Most group trips only accommodate 5-7 writers, with at least 90-100 writers applying. It is similar to an audition or casting call. You will need an assignment letter, previously published clips, and possibly your resume.

Do I have to pay to get on a press trip?

NO! You should not pay for an assignment letter, you should not have to pay for the actual assignment, and you should not have to pay for your press trip. However, keep in mind that some publications do not accept subsidized trips. Some large publications have a "don't ask, don't tell" policy, or a policy of no subsidized trips. If in doubt, ask for a media rate or pay full price.

I'm going on my first press trip and I am nervous. Are there any tips?

Funny you should ask. Keep reading for Press Trip Etiquette.

What should I pay for?

If you are on a comped trip, you are responsible for tipping drivers, tour guides, maid service, concierge, etc. You are usually responsible for room service charges (unless stated otherwise), phones charges, batteries, souvenirs, and other incidentals. Also, be prepared to pay for your activities if given "free" time. It is also a nice gesture to offer to buy the PR or hotel rep a cocktail or similar substitute or to pick up a cab fare, although it's not required.

No matter how you travel, it's still you going

Jeff Goldblum

I think I was invited on my first press trip by mistake. Whatever the reason, it was a blessing. I had no idea what a press trip was. I was dabbling in writing by freelancing with a local newspaper and had aspirations of being the next Danielle Steele (I still do). Somehow, some way, I had an email from a New York public relations firm. I have no idea how they got my contact information, but I wasn't questioning.

The email was an invitation to two Caribbean destinations to experience a resort chain. It sounded like fun, but I didn't know how much it would cost. I called the contact information on the invitation and spoke to the rep. I originally thought it might be a time-share scam. I asked the rep how much it would cost me. She replied that transportation, hotel accommodations, all meals, and activities would be covered. I would be responsible for gratuity and incidentals?

I was shocked and dumbfounded. What was the catch? So, I asked the rep what she needed from me. All she needed was the publications I would submit my articles to and the airport I would like to depart from.

I told her that I would send something to my local paper and that I really wanted to write for National

Geographic. I expected her to laugh, but she told me she could help me with contact information and develop a story line for them. I felt like Alice stepping through the Looking Glass.

I was nervous about the entire experience. I would be flying into Jamaica and staying one night before joining the group at the airport to fly to Curacao. I had never even heard of Curacao before. I had a two year old and a four month old. What was I thinking?

My husband, as always, was very supportive. My parents, on the other hand, were skeptical. To them, if it sounds too good to be true, it usually is. I was still skeptical myself, until the FedEx packet arrived with my plane tickets and itinerary.

I left the US with an over packed suitcase and disposable cameras. I had sunscreen and big hats, sandals and flip-flops, and no idea what I was in for.

I arrived in Jamaica and went through customs, just waiting to get arrested for traveling alone. I've seen those movies, where the female solo traveler gets put in a foreign prison, getting blamed for illegal activities. I kept waiting to get pulled aside and thrown in the slammer for carrying a container of Shower to Shower, which would of course be mistaken for cocaine. Somehow I made it through without incident.

My check in at the hotel was a cocktail greeting. When I arrived in my room, there was a goodie bag(called a schwag bag – which is full of marketing items and small gifts) on the bed. The table was set with fruit and cheese, along with a chilled bottle of champagne. I had just a little time before the first dinner, so I ran a bubble bath and soaked with a glass of champagne in each hand. I giggled until tears rolled down my cheeks. No one at home would ever believe this.

The entire trip was one of those relaxing on the beach, frozen drink in hand, Reggae music in the background dreams. The itinerary was easy and the dinners were long. Each meal consisted of the chef of the restaurant serving one of each of his dishes. Each course was paired with an outstanding wine. On this trip the dessert was always Tiramisu.

I sat under the stars on the last night of my first press trip and wondered what I had done in life to be so lucky. My feet were in the sand with the waves lapping back and forth tickling my toes. The other writers were so nice to me and the resort was lovely. It was all I could ever dream of.

And then I had to come back home. Ah, the life of a travel writer. Now it was time to write – and get articles published. This is the actual "cost" of a press trip.

Travel teaches toleration.

Benjamin Disraeli

1. Don't expect. Be surprised.

Most group press trips are comped by the sponsoring organization/company. Some parts are not included. The writer is responsible paying: phone calls, gratuities, that razor you forgot, tampons, souvenirs, and any activities done on your own.

2. Don't complain because champagne wasn't waiting you when you arrived.

Not all companies have the budget to seduce writers with gifts. The airfare alone can bankrupt a CVB. I once encountered a writer who couldn't believe there wasn't a bottle of champagne in her room, comped of course.

3. Read your itinerary and do some research prior to the trip.

You will mostly likely know exactly what activities are planned before you arrive for a press trip. This can help you develop story angles or plan your extra time (if any).

4. Drink in moderation.

Sure, it's your first press trip. You can't believe that you were even included...and the drinks are "free"! Trust me; you'll be paying for it the next morning at 7am when the group is ready to leave for a full day of tours and activities. Know your limits. You are representing a publication. Editors don't want to hear about drunken escapades.

5. Bring 20 more business cards than you think you'll need.

6. Pack some sealed snacks. (unless flying abroad)
You'll have some long days. The schedule may state that lunch is at noon, but plan on lunch at 2pm. I always keep something in my pack because I like to eat all the time. Protein bars just don't do it for me.

7. Adopt the motto, "To be early is to be on time. To be on time is to be late."
Have respect for the other writers, and the person putting the trip together. This is not a vacation, it's your job. Be on time and be organized.

8. Anticipate your own needs.
If you are prone to headaches when traveling, bring your own medication. If you get the sniffles, bring your own tissue and cold medication. If you have IBS, bring your own Imodium. These things are hard to find when you are out in the wild.

9. Pack necessities in your carry-on.

This wouldn't be the first time an airline misplaced baggage. I always keep my toiletries, a swimsuit, and a change of clothing in my carry on.

10.   Invest in a disposable rain poncho.
These are available for around $1 at your local market. Buy a $1.50 first aid kit while you're there, too.

11.   Always pack a swimsuit, even when going to the cold places.

12.   Don't have an affair with a fellow traveler.
All the other writers will know, and word will get around. You wouldn't believe what I and my fellow travel writers have heard.

13.   Wear a cheap watch.
You never know when you may need to trade it for your freedom. The same goes for cheap canvas tennis shoes.

14.   Don't discuss previous trips you've been on in front of the coordinator of your current trip.
The world of travel writing is small. Coordinators may know who you are referring to or may feel slighted if their budget doesn't "wow" you like another trip. This is their moment. Let the current trip shine.

15.   Don't discuss politics or religion.

If you decide to discuss these things, refrain from being condescending. Remember, if you are in a foreign country; just don't discuss these things at all.

16.   Let the Trip Coordinator know any dietary concerns BEFORE the actual trip.

They will try and accommodate you, but this is not always possible. Be considerate. If you are a vegetarian and are served meat, just move it aside and say nothing for the moment. Don't make a big fuss, just mention to the coordinator before the next meal. However, if allergies are involved, it is a different situation.

17.   Watch your language.

18.   Go over your itinerary.

If you see that hot air ballooning is on the schedule and you are afraid of heights, let the coordinator know before leaving. He/she may be able to schedule another activity for you. Likewise, if you have trouble walking long distances, don't sign up for an adventure press trip. It's just not fair to the other writers or yourself.

19.   Write handwritten thank you notes to all of your hosts when you return.

If you aren't into hand writing, send an email upon your return, at the very least.

20.   Send copies of printed articles resulting from your press trip to the sponsor or host.

I travel not to go anywhere, but to go. I travel for travel's sake. The great affair is to move.

Robert Louis Stevenson

Tourist Boards and Public Relations Companies

Tourist board and public relations companies can be some of the best resources you will need in the travel industry. These agencies can help provide relevent information to include in your articles, official photos, and they arrange press visits. They can also provide contact information for specific areas of their state.

US State Tourism Departments

Alabama
http://www.touralabama.org/

Alaska
http://www.travelalaska.com/media/index.aspx

Arizona
http://www.arizonaguide.com/pressroom/Default.aspx

Arkansas
http://www.arkansasmediaroom.com/

California
http://www.visitcalifornia.com/state/tourism/tour_homepage.jsp

Colorado
http://www.colorado.com/mediaroom.php

Connecticut
http://www.tourism.state.ct.us/pressroom/default.asp

Delaware
http://www.visitdelaware.com/news_mediaguidelines.htm

Florida
http://media.visitflorida.org/ (offers international media contacts)

Georgia
http://www.georgia.org/PressCenter/

Hawaii
http://www.hvcb.org/media/index.htm

Idaho
http://www.visitidaho.org/news/index.aspx

Illinois
http://www.enjoyillinois.com/illinoismediacenter/

Indiana
http://www.in.gov/tourism/Media info on left hand side of site

Iowa
http://www.traveliowa.com/mediacenter/

Kansas
http://www.travelks.com/s/index.cfm?sid=9

Kentucky
http://www.kentuckytourism.com/media/

Louisiana
http://media.louisianatravel.com/

Maine
http://www.visitmaine.com/media/home.php

Maryland
http://www.mdisfun.org/pressroom/ThePressRoom.html

Massachusetts
http://www.mass-vacation.com/jsp/page.jsp?cat=96

Michigan
http://www.michigan.org/medc/home/media.asp?m=0

Minnesota
http://industry.exploreminnesota.com/ no press room

Mississippi
http://www.visitmississippi.org/press%5Fnews/

Missouri
http://news.visitmo.com/

Montana
http://visitmt.com/ no press room, but links to regions

Nebraska
http://www.visitnebraska.org/pressroom/index.htm

Nevada
http://www.travelnevada.com/news.asp

New Hampshire
http://www.medianh.com/

New Jersey
http://www.state.nj.us/travel/news.html

New Mexico
http://www.newmexico.org/newspro/index.php

New York
http://www.iloveny.com/ no press room

North Carolina
http://www.visitnc.com/press_room.asp

North Dakota
http://www.ndtourism.com/pressRoom/

Ohio
http://www.discoverohio.com/press/

Oklahoma
http://www.travelok.com/mediaProf/index.asp

Oregon
http://www.traveloregon.com/ no press room

Pennsylvania
http://mediaroom.visitpa.com/

Rhode Island
http://www.visitrhodeisland.com/mediaroom/index.aspx

South Carolina
http://www.scprt.com/media-room/media-room-main.aspx

South Dakota
http://mediasd.com/media/mediaservices.asp

Tennessee
http://press.tnvacation.com/

Texas
http://travel.state.tx.us/index.aspx

Utah
http://travel.utah.gov/news_and_media/media_relations/

Vermont
http://www.vermontpressroom.com/

Virginia
http://www.vatc.org/pr.htm

Washington

http://www.wastatepressroom.com/

West Virginia

http://www.wvtourism.com/spec.aspx?pgid=177

Wisconsin

http://agency.travelwisconsin.com/PR/index.shtm

Wyoming

http://www.wyomingtourism.org/cms/index.php?id=119

International Tourist Agencies

Scotland
http://www.allmediascotland.com/

Ireland
http://www.tourismireland.com/corporate/

Assoc. of Nat'l Tourist Offices UK
http://www.tourist-offices.org.uk/

Canadian Newspapers
http://www.interpolatethis.com/phpBB2/viewtopic.php?t=47

Tourist Office Directory Worldwide
http://www.towd.com

*Once these contacts are made you may be asked for referrals – or other writers. If you know someone who produces, then give the marketing person their name. Do not send someone with a less than stellar reputation, as it will reflect on you (i.e. an excessive drinker or complainer).

Articles available online to help with your quest.

Rick Steves has one of the best articles on travel writing:
http://www.transitionsabroad.com/publications/magazine/9707/rick_steves_on_being_a_travel_writer.shtml

Travel Writer L. Peat O'Neal offers sound advice and even has a book in print:
http://www.adventuretravelwriter.com/Breakin.htm

Suite101 offers travel writing tips and articles on breaking into the business:
http://www.suite101.com/article.cfm/travel_writing/43904

Phil Philcox tells about Travel Writing for Fun and Profit: http://www.writerswrite.com/journal/aug98/philcox.htm

Don George tells how he fell into the world of travel writing:
http://www.lonelyplanet.com/columns/traveller_archive/14aug02/traveller_index.htm

These are just a few of many travel writer stories out there. I could list all of them, but then this guide would be 200 pages. As you get further into travel writing you will find your own.

Useful Websites

www.writing.org

Durant Imboden is a veteran travel writer who knows his stuff.

http://www.writersweekly.com

http://www.travelwriters.com

http://www.author.co.uk

http://www.writerswrite.com

http://www.guidebookwriters.com

http://www.rolfpotts.com

http://www.mediakitty.com

http://www.writtenroad.com

http://www.fwointl.com/

http://gotravelnews.com

http://www.travelpublicityleads.com

Write down website usernames and passwords on this page.

Organizations *

ASTW   Australian Society of Travel Writers
http://www.astw.org.au

Travel Media Assoc of Canada
http://www.travelmedia.ca

International Food, Wine, and Travel Writers Association
http://www.ifwtwa.org/

New Zealand Writer Groups
http://www.authors.org.nz/info_for_writers/writing_groups.htm

Left Coast Writers
http://www.leftcoastwriters.com/

Bay Area Travel Writers
http://www.batw.org/

American Society of Journalists and Authors
http://www.asja.org/

Canadian Association of Journalists
http://www.eagle.ca/caj/

International Motor Press Association
http://www.impa.org/

National Association of Black Journalists
http://www.nabj.org/

National Association of Hispanic Journalists
http://www.nahj.org/home/home.shtml

National Writers Union
http://www.nwu.org/nwu/

Society of American Travel Writers
http://www.satw.org/satw/index.asp

The Explorers Club
http://www.explorers.org/index.php

National Association of Women Writers
http://www.naww.org/

Writers and Photographers Unlimited
http://www.wpu.org.uk/

Guidebook Writers
http://www.guidebookwriters.com

*Please note: Some of these societies require numerous clips. Some only require one or two. There are at least three here that jury writers and are a little difficult to join. Even so, belonging to at least one or two will help you.

Certainly, travel is more than the seeing of sights; it is a change that goes on, deep and permanent, in the ideas of living.

Miriam Beard

Conferences Can Enhance Your Career

There are travel conferences all year around in different areas of the world. Some can cost big bucks, whereas others are sponsored and cost little to nothing. I have listed many, but if there are any missing from my list, please email me so that I can add them for future travel writers.

Travel Media Showcase – http://www.travelmediashowcase.com This conference occurs annually in the fall and at a different location each year. It offers pre- and post- familiarization trips, as well as networking opportunities and appointments with destination reps. Travel writer Hillary Easom has dubbed this event as "speed dating for travel writers."

I've attended this particular gathering numerous times. Writers are accepted based on availability and expertise. They are responsible for getting to the conference, but will be reimbursed up to $150 for travel expenses. Accommodations, meals, and onsite tours are included in the conference. It was a beneficial experience for me. I made new contacts with CVBs and other writers. I also made some new lifelong friends. I highly recommend Travel Media Showcase.

GoMedia – http://www.gomediacanada.com This is Canada's Premier Conference and is organized by the Canadian Tourism Commission. All expenses, save incidentals, are covered by GoMedia.

World Travel Mart – http://www.wtmlondon.com This consumer and travel trade event occurs in early November each year in London's ExCel Centre. It is the biggest travel show of the year. You won't get a sponsor for your room and board, but it is well worth the contacts you will make for future editorial needs. It is the largest travel show in the world. There are set days for media/press attendees before the show is open to the public.

Photography

When taking photographs where a person is recognizable, you will need a photo release form. I have included links to online examples that you can print out or use as a template. I suggest making your own pocket-size mini release forms to carry wherever you go. They will come in handy. As a travel writer, you may be able to gain access to many places unaccessible to the general public. Be sure to get permission BEFORE you photograph these types of areas.

MODEL RELEASE

In exchange for consideration received, I hereby give permission to [your name here] to use my name and photographic likeness in all forms and media for advertising, trade, and any other lawful purposes.

Print Name:

Signature:

Date:

If Model is under 18: I, _____, am the parent/legal guardian of the individual named above, I have read this release and approve of its terms.

Print Name:

Contact Information:

Signature:

Date:

Model releases available online:

http://www.dpcorner.com/all_about/releases.shtml

http://www.sensuousline.com/forms/adultlon.htm

I suggest investing in a good digital camera. Most editors want photos along with the article. Some of the major magazines have staff photographers, so pictures are not an issue, but with newspapers and regional magazines, it helps sell your story.

A good rule to remember is that it is not the size of the camera that counts, but what you do with it.

Courses:

This guide should not take the place of any course. In fact, I recommend furthering education at all points in life. I, personally, did not take a travel writing course. However, I was fortunate enough to have a good friend in the newspaper business who majored in journalism. Some of the tips he gave me are:

Go out and purchase the Associated Press or Chicago Style books.

The Associated Press and Chicago have a high writing standard.

K.I.S.S.   (Keep It Simple, Stupid)

The majority of the US read on a tenth grade high school level or lower. For international readers, tenth graders are 15 years old. So, keep your wording simple. No need to write *discumbobulated* when you meant *confused*.

Read out loud.

If what you have written makes sense when read out loud, you are doing fine. Try reading it out loud to a friend to see if they understand the article.

Write in YOUR voice.

You are special and unique. No one else is like you. Use this to your advantage. Don't try to be Shakespeare when you are Faulkner. Put personality into your articles.

There are online courses and local university courses that will benefit a travel writer or journalist. You need to learn to be a writer before you can be a travel writer. If you don't have the bones, or the basics of the craft, then it will be a very tough road for you. Take a beginner freelance course or creative writing to get your grammar and style skills honed.

Look also into taking a course at your local community college. The classes sometimes run around $200US and are phenomenal.

Read every travel magazine you can get your hands on. Read newspapers, too.

I travel in so many different ways; I travel high, I rough it....it all depends on who I travel with.

Diane von Furstenberg

Packing Tips for Travel Writers

The most important rule when packing, is to bring what you can carry yourself. You may find yourself in a situation where there may not be anyone to assist you with all your bags.

You should go over your itinerary prior to packing, this way you can get any questions answered before you depart. Also, check the weather forecast to see if you will need warm or cool clothes.

I try to pack clothes that coordinate and are easy to care for. TravelSmith offers these types of outfits in a sturdy, anti-wrinkle fabric. They offer both men's and women's clothing in a variety of styles. Most of their garments are easy to wash while traveling and are quick to dry. www.travelsmith.com

Check all camera equipment and writing implements. Make sure you have plenty of film or memory cards and batteries with chargers. If traveling international, you will need a plug converter.

I also make sure I have a small first aid kit, a pocket-sized rain pancho, and sturdy walking shoes.

Notebooks and pens are a must. I keep a small notepad in my purse or pocket and take notes during my tours or walks. (You will need to find the best way for you to research.)

Sometimes I just take in the sites and don't take notes. Other times I use my camera to take notes by taking pictures of historical markers or signs on entrances.

Insurance

It is advisable to secure trip insurance for your international trips. TravelGuard is one, but there are many others. Most health insurance plans do not cover medical emergencies outside of the US (for US writers). TravelGuard and other similar companies, offer emergency care insurance, medical evacuation, and a variety of other policies to cover unforeseen events. The rates are usually very reasonable.

Press Trip Story:

I was in Brazil on a group press trip. One of our activities included a horseback ride to the beach through a jungle. I was the last one to get a horse, so I was given the one no one else wanted. I could tell she was skittish and not happy, but I got on.

We rode the horses in a line down a trail. Mine kept wanting to stop and eat or get ahead of everyone to get to the beach first. I kept her under control, but when the horse behind us nudged her behind, she got ticked off and started bucking.

My horse kicked the one behind us, which in turn made that horse decide to join in the bucking contest. The other writer fell off her horse onto the hard packed ground. She broke her arm. Of course, I felt bad. No wonder no one else wanted to ride my horse.

Fortunately, the other writer had a TravelGuard policy, which covered her trip to the hospital. I highly recommend a travel medical policy. You never know what can happen.

Travel is very subjective. What one person loves, another loathes.

Robin Leach

Citizen Journalism - Start a Blog

A Blog (short for web log) can serve as an online diary or a place for you to write about travel. You can write about the business of writing. You can write about your family. You can write about anything you want. It's yours to do as you will.

Don't expect to become famous from your blog, though. Recent statistics have stated that there are more blogs out in cyberspace than there are readers. That's okay. A blog can be a very good tool in training yourself to write every day or to become an expert on your area. Keep in mind, though, anything you write on a blog will be visible to the world. The best part is, most blogs are FREE!

Here are a few examples of travel writers blogs:

http://writetotravel.blogspot.com - The beginning of a travel writer's career

http://blogs.bootsnall.com/Seafarer/ - A Family Travel blog

http://vagablogging.net/ - Rolf Potts, successful travel writer

Here are a few links to blogging services:

http://www.blogger.com

http://www.iblog.com

http://www.wordpad.com

http://www.typepad.com

http://www.blogline.com

http://www.blogit.com

Major websites such as MSN.com, Yahoo, and AOL
also offer blogging services for their members.

Once the travel bug bites there is no known antidote, and I know that I shall be happily infected until the end of my life.

Michael Palin

Conclusion

Travel writing is not always a glamorous job. Sometimes you may find yourself in an environment that you are not used to. Even so, it can provide opportunities to experience events and places we would never have dreamed of. I know I pinch myself every day and wonder how I arrived at this place in my life.

My friends call me "International Woman of Mystery", and sometimes I feel like I am living a double life. By day, I am wife, mother, and employee. By night I am Shannon Hurst Lane, travel writer. It sure makes life exciting, for a small town Louisiana gal.

I use myself as an example, because if I can do this, anyone can. Not only have I visited extraordinary destinations, but I have made wonderful life-long friends and I have encouraged friends in my community to see the world beyond their back door. I set up the websiteTraveWriterTips.com and wrote this book as a practical resource for aspiring travel writers.

I like to help people. It is as simple as that. So, I hope, with this book you can pursue your goals as a travel writer. Look for my next book, "Record Keeping for Travel Writers".

Shannon Hurst Lane is a freelance travel writer whose work has appeared in newspapers and magazines around the world. She was a US Correspondent for BBC Radio during Hurricane Katrina and has appeared on various television shows providing travel advice for consumers.

She resides in south Louisiana with her husband, two children, and her mixed breed dog, Sargeant Pepper.

Shannon can be found traveling the globe in search of destinations for others to visit.

You can visit her website at www.shannonlane.com.

www.ingramcontent.com/pod-product-compliance
Lightning Source LLC
Chambersburg PA
CBHW031522040426
42445CB00009B/357